D0108374

August 2000

Dear Jen & Nelson

I wish you all
the love, happiness, & joy...
always. You're a perfect pair!
Love you both,

Ping☺

P.S. You are both
beautiful people and
May you love each
other forever.

WHAT WE DO FOR LOVE

Also by Ilene Beckerman
LOVE, LOSS, AND WHAT I WORE

WHAT WE DO FOR LOVE

written and illustrated by
ILENE BECKERMAN

ALGONQUIN BOOKS OF CHAPEL HILL 1997

Published by
ALGONQUIN BOOKS OF CHAPEL HILL
Post Office Box 2225
Chapel Hill, North Carolina 27515-2225

a division of
Workman Publishing
708 Broadway
New York, New York 10003

For permission to use quotations from copyrighted works, grateful acknowledgment
is made to the holders of copyright, publishers, or representatives named on page
144, which constitutes an extension of this copyright page.

Library of Congress Cataloging-in-Publication Data
Beckerman, Ilene, 1935–
What we do for love/written and illustrated by Ilene Beckerman.
    p. cm.
    ISBN 1-56512-180-5
    1. Beckerman, Ilene, 1935–. 2. Women—United States—Biography. 3. Jewish
women—United States—Biography. 4. Man-woman relationships—United States.
5. Love—United States
I. Title.
HQ1413.B394A3   1997
306.7—dc21   97-16640
                                                                    CIP

10 9 8 7 6 5 4 3 2

Dedicated to
Frank Sinatra,
Burt Lancaster,
and
Stanley

It has taken me a long time to realize that men are neither heroes nor villains, but just people. That's why I have portrayed the men in my past as composites. I have also changed names and identifying details to protect privacy. Everything else I wrote is true, however, especially about how hard it is to find love.

WHAT WE DO FOR LOVE

I love you. I've loved you since the first moment I saw you.
I guess maybe I loved you even before I saw you.
    —Montgomery Clift to Elizabeth Taylor
        in *A Place in the Sun,* 1951

When I was growing up, everyone in the movies I saw found true love. But even Elizabeth Taylor, Debbie Reynolds, and Ingrid Bergman had trouble finding true love in real life. Mr. Right kept turning into Mr. Wrong. For me, too.

On the one hand, I was looking for undying love and an almost perfect person beside me in bed, even though my grandmother once told me, "Stop looking for Prince Charming, Cinderella's already got him."

On the other hand, I never felt pretty enough or confident enough to think any man could be attracted to me once he saw me without makeup.

When I look back on the things I did for love, I don't know whether to laugh or cry.

CHAPTER 1

It was 1950. I was fifteen, and crazy about Frank Sinatra. Frank was crazy about Ava Gardner. They hadn't even gotten married and already they were having big problems. My big problems were just about to start. Up until that time, I'd been in love several times myself, but that was the summer I fell in love with Jeffrey.

Jeffrey was sixteen and the handsomest boy I had ever seen, even better looking than Montgomery Clift. Jeffrey liked my best friend, Dora. When Dora stopped liking him, he paid attention to me, though I was shy, never said anything, and wasn't as pretty as Dora.

That summer I was a waitress in a sleep-away camp in Port Jervis, New York. It was the third summer my grandparents had sent me there. They didn't know what to do with me summers after my mother died and my father left. Jeffrey was a junior counselor at a fancy camp in Maine that had horseback riding and tennis. I was surprised to get a postcard from him:

DEAR GIN,
CAMP's OKAY, BUT WISH
YOU WERE HERE –
ALL MY SOCKS ARE
DIRTY.
        JEFF

GINGY EDELSTEIN
CAMP LEJWIN
PT. JERVIS, NY
            WAITRESS

I didn't mind what he said about the socks. He was so handsome, I would have washed them.

I answered his postcard with a postcard. It took me two days to think of what to say and hours practicing my hand-writing so it would look good. Jeffrey didn't answer.

Since I went to an all-girls high school, it was hard to find boyfriends. Dora went to a coed private school and had a lot.

Fall came. One Saturday afternoon Jeffrey called me and asked if I wanted to see a movie that night.

We went to a double feature at Loew's 72nd Street. *The Glass Menagerie*, with Jane Wyman and Kirk Douglas, was playing with a Western.

I was hoping we would sit in the balcony. I wasn't going to wear my glasses anyway. We necked through half

of the feature and all of the Western. I couldn't believe how lucky I was to be with someone as handsome as Jeffrey.

After the movies, Jeffrey walked me home. When he said good night, he did the most romantic thing: he kissed my hand.

In my room, I turned on the radio. It was always set on WNEW, ready for Martin Block and "The Milkman's Matinee." Martin Block loved Sinatra, too. I lay in bed listening to Sinatra sing "Too Marvelous for Words." I thought about Jeffrey and about cutting bangs and growing my hair long like Jane Wyman's in the movie.

October, November, and December were boring. I didn't have a date for New Year's Eve. But my horoscope in the *New York Mirror* said the new year would be lucky for me, and it was. Jeffrey called me at 9 P.M. on January 6. He said he had to see me.

My grandparents owned a stationery store and we lived above it. Their apartment took one whole floor above the store. I had a small room on another floor. It wasn't hard to sneak out.

Jeffrey met me in the downstairs hall where my grandfather stacked the Sunday newspapers. We hid behind the *Herald Tribune*s and the *Journal American*s and necked standing up, for about an hour and a half. We didn't get caught.

Just before he left, he kissed my hand.

When I got back to my room, I picked up the autographed picture of Sinatra I got for three Lucky Strike
cigarette wrappers and fifteen cents, and turned on the
radio. Frank was singing "Night and Day." I thought he must
feel about Ava the way I felt about Jeffrey. I sang along,

". . . in the silence of my lonely room I think of you."

I didn't hear from Jeffrey again until June 10. I was at Dora's, helping her get ready for a prom with a boy from a fancy prep school. She was trying to squeeze into a merry widow. She'd discovered Sara Lee cream cheese cake the week before.

The phone rang. It was Jeffrey. He asked Dora if she had a date that night. Dora told him I was there. "Tell Gingy I'm not going back to camp," he said. "I'm going to hitch down to Florida. I'll send a postcard." I was so happy Jeffrey was going to write to me that I wasn't so jealous of Dora's prom dress.

I had to go back to camp as a waitress again that summer. On our day off, I went with a friend to see *An American in Paris*. I was glad I could wear my glasses. I moved Gene Kelly above Montgomery Clift on my list of favorite movie stars. I thought about cutting my hair short and curling it like Leslie Caron's in the movie.

During the last week of camp, I finally got a postcard. It had a picture of Miami Beach and said, "It's about 110 degrees in the shade here. See you soon. Love, Jeff."

Fall came. I had a boyfriend I didn't like, Steve. I let him put his tongue in my mouth while I thought about Jeffrey.

Dora told me Jeffrey had called her. I was jealous but didn't tell her. I called his house several times but hung up whenever somebody answered. The more I longed for Jeffrey, the more I let Steve do with me. I had to buy Pan-Cake makeup to cover up the hickeys on my neck.

Dora and I had worked out a code so we could talk on

the telephone and her parents and my grandmother wouldn't
know what we were talking about.

The Code

One: a kiss
Two: necking
Three: petting above the waist
Four: petting below the waist
Five: going all the way

Three and four were only on the girl, of course.
We never thought about touching IT. We never went
past two. Somebody said Joan Brody had fived but we
couldn't believe it. Once I threed with Steve in the balcony of RKO 58th Street but only on the outside of my
pink angora sweater. I never told Dora.

Months went by. I had to write a term paper in my
English class on any author I liked. I wrote my paper on
Dorothy Parker. She knew exactly how I felt. I kept rereading
"A Telephone Call," while I sat by the phone waiting to hear
from Jeffrey.

*Please, God, let him telephone me now. Dear God,
let him call me now. I won't ask anything else
of You, truly I won't. It isn't very much to ask. It
would be so little to You. God, such a little,
little thing.*

Then one night Jeffrey really called. He said he was going away to college. "Will I ever hear from you again?" I asked. "Sure," he said.

He sent me this postcard from Bowdoin:

I broke up with Steve. Dora got me blind dates with her private-school friends. Most of the boys she fixed me up with were rich but had big noses or bad breath or blackheads or still wore braces. I was always hoping for someone handsome.

When it was time for me to choose a college, I wanted to go to Bowdoin, but I got a scholarship to a small school in Boston, another all-girls school. Dora told me Jeffrey would also be in the Boston area. He'd been accepted by Harvard as a transfer student for his sophomore year. They wanted him for the crew team. My prayers had been answered.

Jeffrey called during Freshman Orientation Week and asked me to go to the movies. When he picked me up at the dorm, I could tell that my new college friends were jealous seeing me with someone so good looking.

We went to see *Roman Holiday*. I thought Gregory Peck was really sexy, but even without my glasses, I could see that Audrey Hepburn's eyebrows were too thick. We sat in the balcony and necked.

Jeffrey started to call me for Friday-night dates. Saturday nights he played basketball. I used that time as a beauty night—shaved my legs, did my nails, experimented with different hairstyles.

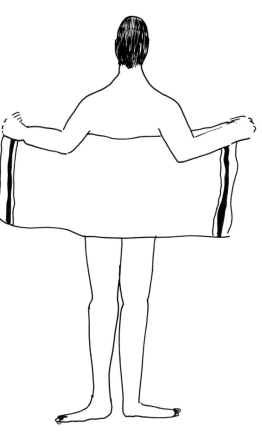

One Friday night I was in Jeffrey's room in Elliot House. We'd been necking and he said he wanted to take a shower. Fine with me, I needed to redo my makeup.

Just as I was putting on my last layer of Maybelline black

cake mascara, Jeffrey walked into the bedroom with nothing on. *Nothing!*

I had no brothers. I could hardly even remember my father's face. I don't think my grandfather ever took off his long underwear. I had never seen a naked boy before. I tried not to look. Jeffrey just laughed.

I had seen parts of a penis. Twice. Once, when I was sitting in a movie, a man sat down next to me. He started breathing heavily and squirming. I kept my eyes on the screen, but I heard him unzip his pants. I knew something bad was going to happen. I never went to a movie alone again.

Another time, I was on a crowded subway car and felt
somebody rubbing up against me. I couldn't move until we
came to the next station. Sideways I saw the penis but I
never saw the face that went with it. After that I always saved
some of my allowance for taxis.

One night, soon after coming out of the shower with no
clothes on, Jeffrey took me back to my dorm after a date.
Boys weren't allowed in our rooms, so we lingered outside. It
was a dark night. We were standing against the side of the
building when he knelt down and put his head and hands
under my skirt. I was scared but let him do it.

He sent me this note the next day:

> I DREAMT ABOUT YOU LAST NIGHT.
>
> IT WAS VERY NICE - BUT SO SHORT A DREAM.
>
>   JEFF

I wrote to Dora. She was at Sarah Lawrence.

October 23, 1954

Dear Dora,

    Good morning.One month of classes gone by.

    I'm taking Intro to Sociology and madly in love with my professor. Everybody thinks he looks like an ape, but I think he's sexy. He used to take out a senior.

    Do you still love Jeffrey? He asks me to the movies sometimes. I know he likes you more than me, but I believe in friendship above all--HA HA!

P.S. I have bags under my eyes this big →

Gingy

Boston was very cold. I'd freeze at football games I wouldn't have enjoyed even if I had worn my glasses or been warm. Boys who go to Ivy League schools don't seem to get cold in the winter. Jeffrey would walk across Harvard Yard in freezing weather wearing just a tweed jacket, his tie floating over his shoulder in the wind.

Sometimes we'd walk around Cambridge, holding hands, not talking, kissing in doorways. Other times we'd play King of the Hill on the steps of Widener Library. He always won.

During winter break, we'd walk around New York, holding hands, not talking, kissing in doorways. One night we walked from the Village, up Fifth Avenue, past Lord & Taylor to F.A.O. Schwarz, looking at the holiday windows. Jeffrey bought me chestnuts and gave all his change to Santa Claus. I was so happy, I felt like a Christian.

CHAPTER 2

Every time we'd go out, Jeffrey kept begging me to go "all the way." One night he told me he couldn't see me anymore because just necking was too painful.

I didn't know any girls who'd done it. I didn't even think I'd know how. No matter how much I loved him, I was too afraid.

Our last date, Jeffrey said, would be to the Dartmouth Winter Carnival. We drove to Hanover with two boys who had a car. It was a long drive. I didn't have anything to say, so I pretended I was sleeping.

Girls weren't allowed in the Dartmouth dorms past 5 P.M., so some local farm families made extra money by letting dates sleep in their homes. Jeffrey left me off at the house where I was to stay. Other girls were staying there, too. I saw their pastel formals, but I never saw them.

An hour later, Jeffrey picked me up to go to a fraternity party. It was very crowded. Jeffrey went to drink beer with his Dartmouth friends. I sat on the floor, next to somebody who had already passed out, and pretended to be bored. I kept going to different bathrooms so I'd have something to do.

After a long time, Jeffrey said he was going to drive me back to the house where I was supposed to sleep because he

was going out with his friends. I told him I didn't want to sleep there, I wanted to spend the night with him. He asked me if I was sure.

We went back to his friend's dorm, but there was a guard at the entrance. I saw somebody throw some stuff out a side window—a parka, snow pants, boots, and gloves. I put them on and pulled the hood up over my face. Jeffrey told me to take off my makeup. I rubbed off only a little lip-

stick. Then I walked right past the guard, in the middle of a group of boys.

Jeffrey's friend gave us his room. I let Jeffrey do it that night. I knew he would know how. He'd often told me he'd been with hundreds of girls and women since he'd hitched to Florida. He didn't even know the names of some, he said.

After it was over, I thought: I won't have clean underpants to wear in the morning, but that's okay because Jeffrey will love me now.

That's when I found out that in sex, once you do something, you have to keep doing it. At the end of my freshman year, I thought I was pregnant. I told Jeffrey. He told me he had to go someplace and had to leave Boston.

I didn't know what to do. My friends were all virgins, they said. I was afraid to tell the school nurse. I thought I'd be expelled or, worse, she'd tell my grandparents. Then I thought about the Professor. I had been in his Introduction to Sociology class first semester, and his Marriage and the Family class second semester. I thought he knew so much about life that I could trust him. I made an appointment to see him. It was the right decision. He took me to a doctor. I wasn't even pregnant.

Maybe if I had been prettier, Jeffrey wouldn't have left.

Maybe my grandmother was right, "If a man can't keep his pants up, he's sure to let you down."

CHAPTER 3

When I got back to school in the fall, I saw the Professor walking up the library steps as I was going down. He smiled at me and asked how my summer had gone. "Fine," was all I said.

My college held acquaintance dances a few times a year, inviting boys from the neighboring Boston colleges. The prettiest, most popular girls never went. I went.

I was surprised to see the Professor as chaperone at one of the acquaintance dances. At 6'4" tall, he stood out. I'm 5'8", but I usually wore flats to acquaintance dances because so many short boys went. I ran back to my dorm and put on my highest heels.

I thought he looked at me a few times, but I made believe I didn't see him. When he got up, walked in my

direction, and stood in front of me, I couldn't look up.
"Would you like to dance?" he asked.

    He put his hand around my waist and pulled me close.

He was grinning. We started to dance a slow fox-trot. I felt like Ginger Rogers dancing with Fred Astaire, only taller.

The next Friday, I found this note on the message board at school:

```
Dear Ilene,
      Would you like to see the John Marin
exhibition at the Boston Museum today? I'm
going to buzz over during the 7th period. If
you'd like to come, be in my office as
close to 1:45 as possible.
                              H.
```

I got to his office at 1:44. I almost didn't go because I had my period and my face was broken out. I hardly said a word the entire afternoon. I didn't even know what to call him. As we walked through the exhibition, he stood in back of me and told me all sorts of facts about John Marin and watercolors. By the time we got to the last painting, he was standing so close I could smell his cigarette breath.

The next day I left a watercolor I had painted of my impressions of the Marin show on his desk.

This is the note he left for me:

```
Dear Ilene,
     Your Marin is exquisite--a wonderful
combination of symbols and representation, a
rich composition whose integrity is achieved
with admirable economy of means.
     It has so much spontaneous dash I can
hardly believe it isn't an original. If I
hadn't had my eyes on you most of the time,
I'd suspect you of slipping one under your
coat.
                         H.
```

I wasn't in any of the Professor's classes sophomore year. His office was right near the main entrance and he kept the door open. If I thought I looked good, I walked by as often as I could but didn't look in. When my face was broken out, I took the long way around.

A few weeks went by and nothing happened. I wondered who Jeffrey was dating. One Saturday night I was in my dorm playing honeymoon bridge with another girl who didn't have a date when the intercom buzzed. I had a phone call. I went out to the hall where the phone was, said "Hello," and recognized the Professor's voice.

"Would you like to go dancing with me one night?" he asked.

"Yes," was all I said.

"Good. I'll pick you up at seven o'clock next Friday. Don't eat. We'll have some dinner together."

I was embarrassed to tell my friends I was going on a date with the Professor. They thought he was weird.

Everybody knew he dated students. A different one every year. Only seniors. Only tall ones. Usually natural blonds. I wasn't a senior and I had recently dyed my hair as dark as Elizabeth Taylor's.

A girl in my dorm had seen the Professor perform in a modern-dance recital in Cambridge. She said he did a dance with a large garbage can. He got in the can, stuck out his foot, his arm, his head, then climbed in and out of the can. All through high school I'd taken lessons at the New Dance Group on 59th Street. I thought his choreography sounded great.

Everyone made fun of him because he was so tall and thin and sat cross-legged on top of his desk when he was teaching.

I thought he was handsome. As handsome as Rex Harrison, Abraham Lincoln, and Arthur Miller (but better looking than Arthur Miller). I didn't mind his gray hair.

He had beautiful hands and long fingers that looked as if he could play the piano, but he couldn't.

I tried to look sophisticated the night of our date. I pinned my ponytail into a French twist like Grace Kelly's. I borrowed a black crepe de chine sheath from a girl in my dorm, wore pearl teardrop earrings, lots of Shalimar, four-inch heels and was ready by six.

The buzzer rang at seven. "There's a man waiting for

you," the girl on duty yelled into the phone. My friends ran to the lobby to get a good look at him and came back to the room howling with laughter. I thought they were just getting back at me because they were still jealous about Jeffrey. I couldn't wait to get into the Professor's dark-blue Dodge.

We didn't talk in the car. We went to a restaurant where you could dance called the Meadows, in Framingham, about a twenty-minute drive from Boston. I still have a matchbook from there.

It wasn't very crowded for a Friday night. He ordered a martini and asked what I wanted to drink. I usually ordered a brandy alexander. But I didn't think that was a sophisticated enough drink. "A daiquiri, please," I said. Patricia Neal drank daiquiris in *The Fountainhead*.

I was glad when we got up to dance so I didn't have to talk. The vocalist tried to sing "Embraceable You" like Sinatra. He even wore a bow tie.

When the waiter asked for our dinner order, I got what he got—pork chops. I'd never tasted them before. My grand-mother wouldn't let me.

He ordered more drinks, finished his pack of cigarettes, and started on mine. We both smoked Pall Malls. He was very complimentary and I blushed several times. I could tell he was having a good time.

We got back to the dorm a little before my midnight curfew. Just as I was about to open the car door, he leaned over and pulled me toward him. I didn't like the smell of his martini/cigarette breath. His hand stroked my hair, then my face, and then moved down the front of my dress. Now I knew what Sinatra meant when he sang about chills up his spine.

We started to go out regularly. The Professor always made the plans. We'd eat in Chinatown, see foreign films at the Brattle Theater in Cambridge, go to concerts at Symphony Hall. I'd never heard a live symphony orchestra before. Or heard of his favorite singer, Elisabeth Schwartzkopf. Most of the time we just went to his apartment, two rooms on Mass Ave in Cambridge. He'd mark papers and I'd do my homework.

I still couldn't call him by his first name. I didn't know why he kept asking me out. One evening I asked him. "You're very original and more attractive than you think," he said, "—or than I deserve." I turned red. No one had ever complimented me that way.

He didn't touch me again for a long time. One night we were in his apartment and he'd been drinking. He grinned at me over his glasses, came over to the couch, picked me up, and carried me into the bedroom. He kissed me. He undid my clothes. Then he was beside me on the bed. Then on top of me.

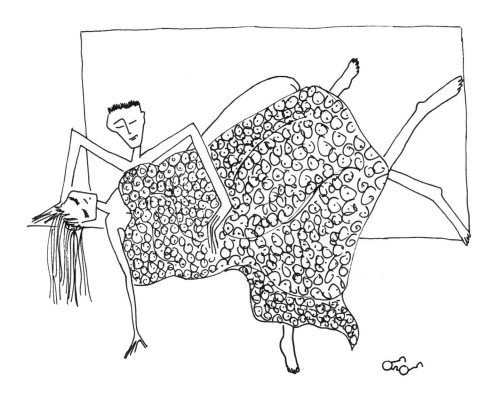

It was over quickly. The Professor said it was time for me to go back to my dorm. I got dressed. When I went into the other room, he was reading.

"I've just finished this," he said. The book was Robert Anderson's play *Tea and Sympathy*. He turned to the last page and read, "Years from now . . . when you talk about this . . . and you will . . . be kind."

CHAPTER 4

I had almost stopped thinking about Jeffrey, so I was surprised to find an envelope from him in my mailbox at the dorm. Inside was a love poem with lots of adjectives.

Harvard had turned him into Robert Browning.

I wondered if he had put the envelope in my mailbox by mistake, but I kept it.

One of my friends told me she'd seen Jeffrey at a party with a girl who was all over him.

The next week there was a letter that ended, "All I can do is pray it's you whenever the phone rings. I think of you constantly. Someday it has to happen."

I'd spent years praying to hear those words from Jeffrey. Wished on hundreds of stars and on every

chicken and turkey wishbone. Why now?
I wondered if he knew about the Professor.

CHAPTER 5

One night I was at the Professor's when he put his book down, looked at me over his glasses, and asked, "When are we getting married?"

I didn't say anything. I never thought anybody would want to marry me. Especially someone like the Professor. My Uncle Larry had told me years ago that nobody would ever marry me because I didn't wear my retainer when my braces came off.

The Professor never mentioned marriage again, but a few weeks later he said he had a friend who sold diamonds wholesale and we should go and pick one out. He made an appointment for an actual day and time.

I chose a one-carat solitaire in a platinum setting.

I told my friends in the dorm that the Professor and I

were going to be married. My two close friends asked me if I was sure I knew what I was doing. The other girls asked me a lot of questions I didn't want to answer.

I was scared to tell my grandparents. I was twenty and the Professor was thirty-seven. Lauren Bacall was twenty and Bogart forty-five when they got married; Mia Farrow was twenty and Sinatra fifty when they got married. But neither Lauren nor Mia were Harry and Lillie Goldberg's granddaughter.

The Professor also wasn't Jewish. Was I looking for trouble!

I kept putting off telling my grandparents, but the Professor said I had to. I wrote a letter. My grandfather called and said I was killing my grandmother. My grandmother wouldn't get on the phone. I couldn't wait to get off.

At the end of sophomore year, we were married at the Professor's friend's home in Dobbs Ferry, New York. The Professor was born a Catholic but never went to church. He said he had more affinity for the ethical beliefs of Judaism. My grandparents were not impressed.

One of his friends was a Reform rabbi in Westport, Connecticut, and performed the service. As he said the prayers in Hebrew, the Professor answered in English: "With this ring you are wedded to me in accordance with the law of

Moses and Israel." I wondered what either one of us was
doing there.

My grandmother came to the wedding. My grandfather
didn't. Just as well. There was no food. Only a wedding cake
with a bell on top and champagne.

We drove back to his apartment in Cambridge that
night. In the car, I wondered to myself how everything had
progressed so quickly. I didn't feel married, but I didn't know
how married was supposed to feel. In the movies, when
Doris Day finally hooked Rock Hudson, she didn't stop
smiling.

The next day I went to my dorm to get my things. I had
only clothes and books, so I took a taxi over. My husband
said I could use his car, but I didn't know how to drive. He
had an extra key made for me to his apartment and had

cleared out one closet. I found this note when I got back from the dorm:

> Ma cherie,
>   When you arrive and recover from your disappointment at not finding the bureaus moved, please call me at my office and I'll explain to you the prospects, the joys and sorrows, frustrations and minor achievements waiting to be worked out this day. I'll also come back quickly.
>
>   H.

I got a letter in the mail from Jeffrey that week. "You are the one object that I have been able to touch with all that I feel," it said. "Do you expect me not to fight for it." I hid the letter in my underwear drawer.

I started to like being married. I didn't have to worry about getting a date or finding someone to play honeymoon bridge with if I didn't have a date. Classmates who had never been friendly started saying hello. All the professors knew my name.

I liked being with the Professor. He never seemed uncomfortable. He always knew how to act and what to say.

He was the smartest person I'd ever known. He was even smart at home. He kept a small photo of Proust on his desk. I kept my autographed photo of Sinatra in my underwear drawer with my other secrets.

Weekend breakfasts were made up of sausage and eggs and Yeats and Wallace Stevens. His favorite Wallace Stevens poem was "Sunday Morning."

He'd read aloud with great feeling, pronouncing every word as if it were a gift he had chosen especially for me.

Complacencies of the peignoir, and late
Coffee and oranges in a sunny chair,
And the green freedom of a cockatoo
Upon a rug mingle to dissipate
The holy hush of ancient sacrifice.

I had absolutely no idea what the poem was about. If he called on me, I wouldn't know the answer.

Rimbaud, Baudelaire, and Rilke shared our dinners.
Sometimes I could see tears in his eyes as he read aloud in
French and in German.

He encouraged me to read. C. P. Snow, Kingsley Amis,
Henry Green. "You'll love Isak Dinesen," he assured me.
Henry Higgins redid Eliza Doolittle. F. Scott Fitzgerald redid
Sheila Graham. The Professor was redoing me.

He taught me how to cook pork roasts, his mother's
way; how to make *Sauerbraten*, the German way; how to
grind coffee beans, the French way; and how to use his
espresso maker, the Italian way.

He told me why Irish whiskey was the best drink,
Johnnie Walker Black Label second, and a dry martini third.

He taught me how to drive. And then he paid for me to
take driving lessons.

We redecorated his apart-
ment without spending much
money. He made about $5,000 a
year and now he had to pay for
me. We cut out Utamaro and
Klee prints from his art books
and put them on the wall,
unframed, in the living room.
We bought wood from a lum-

beryard and metal legs from a hardware store to make a coffee table. We bought new orange canvas for his black butterfly chair and footstool to brighten the room. We didn't have a TV. We didn't need one, he said. He had a good hi-fi.

We were establishing a married-life routine. We read the *Christian Science Monitor* every day. Every night we'd listen to a woman with a British accent read the news on a Cambridge radio station. Every Saturday afternoon he'd play squash with his friend Joe, and Joe's wife would cook broccoli and hard-boiled-egg casseroles for dinner. They all loved that casserole.

The Professor and Joe would inevitably start talking about politics. The Professor was passionate about Adlai Stevenson. He thought being called an egghead was a supreme compliment. Joe was an Eisenhower Republican.

They'd start out joking about the upcoming election. The more they drank, the redder the Professor's face would get and the louder his voice would become. He'd start pacing, waving his arms wildly, spilling his martini. They'd always end up laughing, mixing more martinis, better friends than ever. I couldn't understand it. All the times my grandparents fought and screamed at one another, they never ended up laughing.

One night the Professor and I actually saw Stevenson. We went to a rally at the Boston Garden. Everybody started going crazy, yelling and clapping when Stevenson got up to speak. It was very exciting. After the rally, I called up his Boston headquarters to volunteer and they sent me to Alston to stuff envelopes. I went only once.

We went to the movies a lot, too. We had an agreement. For every film he chose, I could choose the next.

For his Ingmar Bergman's *Wild Strawberries*, I chose Audrey Hepburn and Gary Cooper in *Love in the Afternoon*.

For his Akira Kurosawa's *Seven Samurai*, I chose Leslie Caron and Fred Astaire in *Daddy Long Legs*.

For his Federico Fellini's *La Strada*, I chose Audrey Hepburn and Fred Astaire in *Funny Face*.

I always liked to see how movie ingenues acted with older men.

Leslie   Fred   Audrey   Me

The Professor had a lot of friends. Most of them were professors at Harvard (the Professor had gotten his Ph.D. from Harvard). They got together very frequently to talk and to drink. Once in a while one of them would try to involve me in the conversation but would soon lose interest.

The only way I interacted when we got together was to remove the hand of Dr. Alan Hawthorne from my thigh every time he sat next to me.

I was jealous of some of the Professor's friends' wives who weren't even that pretty but who always knew what to say and danced too close to him at their parties. My grandmother had once told me, "A little charm and you don't have to look like Hedy Lamarr."

CHAPTER 6

I'd heard from Dora that after Jeffrey graduated from Harvard, he joined the navy. So I was surprised when I thought I saw him standing near the front steps as I was leaving school late one afternoon. I had my period and my face was broken out, so I started to go back inside. Too late. He had seen me.

"Gin," he called. "Or should I call you by your married
name?" I didn't say anything, just kept my head down.
"Why did you do it?" I didn't answer.

"I have to be back on ship in a little while. I'll write to
you. I have your address. Be a good girl." He kissed my
cheek, then my hand, and left. He looked more handsome
than ever in his navy uniform.

It reminded me that for a few weeks after my father left,
I'd see him standing in a doorway waiting for me to pass by
on my way to school. I never knew what to say to him after
he said my name. After a while he wasn't there anymore.

CHAPTER 7

The Professor used to get the mail and bring it upstairs. Usually there wasn't anything for me, but one day I saw a letter on the table addressed to me. I recognized the handwriting immediately. It was Jeffrey's. I wondered if the Professor knew. All he said was, "I put a letter for you on the table."

It was a two-page letter about his duties on ship and the weather on the east coast of Africa. It didn't even mention me. I wasn't even going to save it.

I kept getting letters

from Jeffrey from all over the world. The Professor always left them on the table, saying only, "You've got another letter from your friend."

In most of the letters, Jeffrey wrote about navy life. I was always disappointed. Finally a letter came that ended "Someday we'll be together." Even though I knew I couldn't believe him, I wanted to.

I still had my Sinatra LPs, but I didn't play them much. Elisabeth Schwartzkopf's LPs took precedence. After I read the letter, I put on Sinatra. The Professor wasn't home, so I turned up the volume.

The Professor liked me to walk around the apartment without clothes. I was very self-conscious of my bad body parts, but I wanted to please him. When I'd make dinner,

clean, or do my homework in the nude, he'd even put down his book.

When we had sex, he liked me to wear a merry widow and keep my stockings and heels on. When he drank too much, he'd pass out before he finished.

I'd write the Professor love notes and put them in his pockets, on his desk, in his briefcase. He never mentioned them.

Dora wrote me that a girl we knew in high school, who got married the same time I did, was pregnant. I asked the Professor if we could ever have a baby. "I could never be a father," he said. "What if I died when my child was young. I can't bear the thought of it." Then he walked out of the room. He once told me he was twelve when his father died.

I never mentioned it again, but I thought about it. I was busy with school and trying to still be friends with a few girls. It was difficult because we couldn't double-date.

Every time I felt really down about the Professor and me, I'd fantasize about other people's love affairs.

I'd be Garbo being Anna Karenina, wearing a long black coat trimmed with fur, trembling as I begged Vronsky not to leave me.

"Anna, you are all my life to me," he'd say. "You should have known that from the beginning." We were doomed.

Or I'd be Garbo being Camille, whispering to Fredric March, "Let me love you; let me live for you; don't ask more from heaven than that—God might get angry." God got angry.

Or I'd be Merle Oberon clinging to Heathcliff. And he'd be crying, "Cathy, Cathy, you loved me. What right have you to throw love away?" I'd answer him, my arms full of heather, "Heathcliff, make the world stop right here. Make everything stop and stand still and never move again. Make us never change. . . . I'm yours, Heathcliff. I'll never be anyone else's." Then I'd die.

I'd be Ingrid Bergman with Bogart in *Casablanca,* and
Sam would be at the piano playing "As Time Goes By." Then
I'd get on the plane with Paul Henreid.

One afternoon, I got home earlier than usual from
school. The Professor wasn't home yet. There was a letter on
his desk and I read it.

```
Dear Ilene,
     I have been dreading writing this letter.
It is inevitable that I shall doubt the
wisdom of my actions for some time to come.
It's possible that I'll spend the rest of
my life regretting my stupidity.
     But I cannot live with you anymore. . . .
```

The letter stopped in the middle of the page.

I ran out of the apartment. I had nowhere to go. I sat
on a bench at a bus stop on Mass Ave until it got dark.

When I got back to the apartment, I could see a light under the door. He was home. I stood outside the door biting my cuticles. Waiting for something, anything, to happen. The woman who lived in the next apartment came out to throw away her garbage. I didn't want to talk to her, so I opened the door.

He was sitting in his favorite chair, a drink in one hand, a book in the other. "You read the letter on my desk," he said. "I'm sorry you read it. I wasn't ready to send it yet."

I didn't want to hear that. I started to cry.

The Professor got up from his chair and handed me his drink. He made another drink for himself, then lit a cigarette for himself and one for me, just like Paul Henreid did for Bette Davis in *Now, Voyager*.

He told me he'd been in psychoanalysis for fourteen years, and was making progress. Our getting married, he said, had been his analyst's idea. I was nonthreatening, his analyst had said. But, according to the Professor and his analyst, the marriage didn't seem to be working. Of course, he said, he was always very attracted to me. "It's just a mistake," he said, "a mistake."

"It's been difficult for me as well as for you," he said. "Let's just go to sleep now."

He slept far away from me that night, but I didn't care.

I was back in his bed. The crying and whiskey had made me very tired.

For the next few weeks, things went back to normal. We ate pork chops, we went to the movies, and he played squash. We even had sex more than usual. But each time it took less and less time.

Other days, if he had too much to drink, the sex didn't work out. I always thought it was my fault. He'd just turn around and go to sleep. I got used to seeing his long back.

I had to complete a work-study program to get my degree and had been accepted for a six-week internship in New York. I knew the Professor had to teach and wouldn't be able to come with me. "If you could," I asked him one night, "would you come with me?"

"Actually," he said, "I've been looking forward to this time alone."

I was going to stay with Dora, who was now an actress and had an apartment in midtown. I took a Trailways bus to New York on Sunday and started my internship on Monday. The Professor called me Sunday night to see if I got there, Monday night to see how the job was, and then every night. He couldn't have been nicer, funnier, or more encouraging. I started to forget how bad I felt.

The day before I was to return to Boston, I got this letter:

Dear Ilene,

There is no use in my waiting any longer to write to you. It is impossible for me to ask you to come back to me, and I must resolve my present anxiety by getting a divorce. I am desperately sorry; my internal problems frighten me to death and make me feel guilty; my insides are churning; but I have kept us both in this sad state long enough--too long.

There is no chance that I will change my mind. Nothing but more misery for us both would result from any attempt on my part to prolong this period of indecision. It is better for us both to start a new life.

If I write again, it will be only to deal with the practical questions. For example, many of your things are still here.

I cannot tell you how miserable I feel myself.

H.

Dora was away for the weekend. I read the letter over and over, even though I knew it by heart the second time I read it.

I found an almost-full bottle of sherry and a closed bottle of vodka. I gulped down the sherry, went into the bathroom, and started to slash my wrists with a razor Dora shaved her legs with. I tried to make deep cuts, but the razor was dull and full of hair.

The sherry made me nauseous. I wanted to throw up, but all I could do was gag. I sat down and put my head over the open toilet bowl. I must have passed out.

Hours later, I woke up and cleaned the dried blood from my wrists. Even though the cuts were superficial, I had to wear long-sleeved blouses for several weeks.

CHAPTER 9

Going to a psychiatrist wasn't unusual in 1957. I had no money, so I went to a clinic at Columbia-Presbyterian Hospital, hoping they'd refer me to a doctor who would see me for free.

They gave me the names of three doctors. None of them would take me without payment. I took a Trailways bus back to Boston and went right to Mass General Hospital. Maybe they were looking for people to analyze. But to see a psychiatrist for free, I had to sign myself in to the psychiatric ward.

To be admitted, I first had to tell my story to a social worker, then to an admitting physician, then to the floor psychiatrist, and then to the psychiatrist assigned to me. Each time I told my story, I gave more details so I could be admitted.

A nurse asked me if I had laces in my shoes, if I was

wearing a belt, if I had a tweezers, scissors, matches, razor, mirror, or pocketknife on me. Then she asked for my jewelry. I handed over my engagement ring and my wedding band, and I took the silver hoops out of my ears. I could wear my own clothes, she told me.

The ward they put me in was a nonviolent one. The violent ward was down the hall and had a different kind of door, with a small window and bars. Someone told me that every time a loud bell rang, there was trouble in the violent ward. The bell rang infrequently, but when it did, the nurses ran down the hall in a hurry. I thought about one of the Professor's friends who was so brilliant he had to have electric shock treatments.

I met some girls in my ward and didn't know why they were there. They didn't seem so different from the freshmen in my dorm.

I was allowed to use the pay phone in the hall. I called the Professor and told him where I was. "I'm so glad you're getting help," he said. I didn't know why he said that. He didn't even know about my wrists.

Every time I met with my psychiatrist, he'd ask me a lot of questions: What kind of movies did I like? Did I have any hobbies? What books did I read? I didn't think he was much older than I was. He looked like someone

I wouldn't have danced with at an acquaintance dance.

There was an arts and crafts room on the floor that was opened a few hours every day. One day I drew something with crayons that looked like a gargoyle but I quickly tore it up. The face looked too familiar.

A letter was given to me.

```
Dear Ilene,
     At the moment, I am drunk--probably
couldn't write such a letter any other way.
     Please don't come back to the apart-
ment. I have investigated housing for you in
Cambridge and took the liberty of renting
you a room on Chauncy Street, which I will
pay for, for now. I am enclosing the address
and a key.
     As for myself, I don't know what will
happen to me. Despite all irony and unhappi-
ness, I can sincerely sign,

                    Love,
                    H.
```

I showed the letter to my psychiatrist. He asked what I was going to do. I had come to the hospital because I didn't know what to do. Being there, I knew one thing I wanted to do: get out of there!

A woman had come into our ward from the violent one. She had a big bandage around her neck. Someone said she had tried to slash her throat. Every time I looked at her bandaged neck, I thought about how the razor had felt on my wrists. When she sat down at my table for dinner, I couldn't swallow.

A week later, I was discharged from the hospital. Good luck, they said.

I hadn't been in touch with the Professor since I got his letter, but I had the key he sent me to the room on Chauncy Street. I went there. It was a boardinghouse for foreign students. Fine with me, I didn't want to talk to anyone anyway.

I wrote a letter to the Professor. I told him that I was angry that he had used me for his own selfish purposes. I told him I had lost all the love, all the respect I'd had for him. I didn't tell him I still loved him.

When I finished, I put on makeup, took the M.T.A. over to the apartment, and dropped the letter in our mailbox. I had hoped his car would be in the parking lot. It wasn't.

CHAPTER 10

I had missed only three weeks of school, not counting my work-study time. Finals would be starting soon. I wanted to graduate. I wanted to be near the Professor.

I went back to school and told my professors I had been sick. They must have known exactly what kind of sick I was—they were all the Professor's friends. My friends seemed to be staying away from me. There had been rumors.

I didn't want to pass his office. I used the back entrance. If I saw him, I hid. At night I sat by the phone, Dorothy Parker's "A Telephone Call" going round in my head. "Please God, make him call." This time it was the Professor I wanted to call me.

I passed my exams with low C's, good enough to grad-

uate. I didn't go to graduation. As a faculty member, the
Professor would be on the podium.

I hadn't been in touch with my family for a while.
They'd stopped paying my tuition. As a faculty wife, I went
for free. Sometimes when they'd call, the Professor would say
I was fine but I was in the library. I didn't invite them to
graduation. I wrote and said graduation was no big deal.

The afternoon of graduation, I took a Trailways bus to
New York. Dora said I could stay with her for a while. I was
lucky and got a job right away. I made seventy dollars a
week.

Dora kept telling me to get a divorce. She said I was
still young and I could do better. She gave me the name of a
lawyer and I went to see him. We agreed on two things: I
would get a divorce and the lawyer would get $500.

The Professor didn't respond to the lawyer's first letter.
The lawyer wrote again.

I WOULD APPRECIATE YOUR VERY EARLY RESPONSE AS
TO WHETHER YOU PREFER AN AMICABLE SETTLEMENT
TO HAVING THE SAID MATTER LITIGATED BEFORE A
COURT OF COMPETENT JURISDICTION.

I got this letter:

Dear Ilene,
    Please call off your lawyer with his
implied threats. Try not to be too hard on
me in your thoughts. I have not despaired
yet. Despite my unkindness, which though it
sprang from emotional confusion still is
hard to forgive, I know, I do love
you still.
    I think you are better off than I am.
You probably can't forgive me. I wish you
could. I wouldn't blame you if you were not
interested or, worse, if you hated me.
    I feel <u>terrible</u> (but I know you don't
care).
H.

On June 15, 1958, my twenty-third birthday, I flew to Mexico to get a divorce.

I should never have expected anyone as smart as the Professor would be serious about me.

Once I heard my grandmother tell someone, "F.D.R. didn't stay with Eleanor because she was a good kisser."

CHAPTER 11

Dora had kept in touch with Jeffrey. He'd told her he was going to go to law school in Washington, D.C. I didn't tell her that I was still crazy about him.

Dora had gone to Boston to join a repertory theater group. We made an arrangement that I could stay in her apartment, rent free, if I took care of her dog, Greco, a Doberman. One of my responsibilities was to cook him kidneys—definitely one of the foulest-smelling things in the world.

Greco always reminded me of Jeffrey. Great face, lynx eyes, dark hair, muscular body, always ready to hump somebody. And you never knew when either one was going to betray you. There were always stories about people who were last seen walking their Dobermans on a beach. Weeks later, human bones are found. The thing in Jeffrey's favor was I never had to cook him kidneys.

One evening when I came back from walking Greco, I saw

Jeffrey standing in the doorway. I thought he was waiting for
Dora. It was summer. He was tanned and looked very handsome.

He said he just had to look at me. Then he left. It took
all my willpower not to kick Greco.

A few weeks later, he called me at work. I didn't know
how he got the number. He told me he had an apartment in
Washington and I should come down.

I hadn't heard from the Professor since the divorce. I
had no boyfriend and felt like nothing without one. You were
supposed to have a boyfriend, even one you didn't like. Or,
at least you were supposed to be dating. You're nobody till
somebody loves you. I even had the Sinatra record.

Dora had come back from Boston but was always going
to auditions. I didn't fit in with her acting friends anyway.

One Friday I was sleeping when the buzzer started ringing and ringing. Dora was away. Greco started to bark. It was 5 A.M., still dark. I went to the intercom and mumbled, "Who is it?"

"Jeffrey."

I put my thumb on the buzzer and held it there.

He came into the apartment and just said, "Why aren't you in Washington?" Then his arms were around me and he was kissing me. I wished I had brushed my teeth. I wished I was wearing one of Dora's sexy nightgowns instead of my torn one.

I didn't go to work that day. Or call to tell them I wouldn't be in. I never got to brush my teeth. Or put on makeup. Or change my nightgown. I didn't need a nightgown. When Jeffrey left that night, a familiar odor filled the apartment—Greco.

Saturday morning I slept late. No need to take Greco out. The buzzer rang late in the afternoon. I thought it would be Jeffrey. It was a delivery man with flowers. The card said:

* 69 *

You shouldn't get these. In a day they'll be withered and thrown away, and what will you think of me then?
Will you know that I love you, that I will be as earnest in two months as now.

Be brave.   Trust me.

J.

A few weeks later, I was on the Madison Avenue bus going home from work when I looked out the window. There was Jeffrey crossing 53rd Street holding hands with someone. Maybe it was just my imagination.

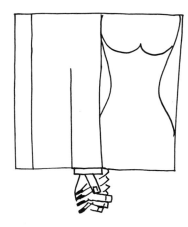

I kept getting letters from him begging me to come to Washington. Our own apartment. No dog.

I wrote back that I'd come down in a couple of weeks, when I got things settled at work. I wrote him that in January, in February, in March, April, and May.

He kept writing.

Maybe this was a new Jeffrey. Maybe I didn't have to be so cautious.

CHAPTER 12

On Saturday, June 15, my birthday, I took a Trailways bus to Washington, D.C. Jeffrey met the bus. He didn't seem to know it was my birthday, so I didn't tell him.

At eight-thirty we went to hear a concert by the U.S. Naval Band on the Potomac, near the Watergate. It was my favorite kind of night. Tennessee Williams hot. The stars were twinkling on the Potomac. The orchestra played excerpts from *Rhapsody in Blue* and *West Side Story*. Jeffrey held my hand. I knew coming to Washington was the right decision. First thing Monday I would look for a job.

After the concert, we went back to his apartment. I looked at the furniture, the dishes, the food in the refrigerator, the clothes hanging in the closet, the inside of the medicine cabinet. Nothing was familiar.

Jeffrey said he was tired so we went to bed. He fell asleep almost the minute he got into bed. I was restless. I wasn't as confident about my decision anymore. I watched the sky turn from dark to dawn. Just as it was getting light, Jeffrey reached out to me and called me Carol.

I was lucky to find a cab so early on a Sunday.

CHAPTER 13

On Monday I was back at Dora's and back at work.
Lunchtime, I called Columbia-Presbyterian Hospital for a
referral.

I was referred to a psychiatrist in a fancy doorman
building on Fifth Avenue, across from the Metropolitan
Museum of Art. He would see me, he said, every other week
for seventy dollars a session. Quite a reduction from his
usual $150 fee, he said. The sessions would last fifty min-
utes. Seventy dollars was one week's pay.

I would go to my appointment, lie down on a brown
leather chaise, and not say a word. My psychiatrist sat in a
black leather chair where I couldn't see him. He didn't say
anything either.

He was always writing in a little notebook. I didn't know

what about since we didn't talk. After three sessions, just to justify spending seventy dollars, I said something. I told him I was very unhappy and didn't know what to do with my life.

After a while, he said, "Did you ever feel like that before?" I wasn't sure I wanted to answer. I didn't like him.

"Yes, I always feel like that."

Neither of us spoke again until the session was over. As I was leaving, he said he would have to postpone next week's meeting since he would be away. I didn't care. Seventy dollars would buy a lot of shoes. Shoes would probably make me feel better than he did, anyway.

I was glad to be seeing a psychiatrist, though. Everybody seemed to be seeing one. Or a diet doctor. But I thought I must be doing something wrong because *nothing was happening* except that I was starting to get behind in my

payments. I didn't want to go anymore. I didn't know if
it was because of the money or because nothing was
happening. I wrote him that I didn't want to continue. He
wrote back.

P .   H E R B E R T   B O W M A N

FOR PROFESSIONAL SERVICES: $490

7 Interviews.

I realize that your present financial circumstances may
not allow prompt payment. I would appreciate hearing
from you as to what arrangements you are making to
take care of this matter.

Two weeks later I heard from him again.

P .   H E R B E R T   B O W M A N

FOR PROFESSIONAL SERVICES: $480

7 Interviews.

The arrangements for payment you suggested are
unsatisfactory. I have only received a total of $10 on
your bill of $490.

P. H. B.

CHAPTER 14

I gave up looking for love and decided to concentrate on getting ahead at work. I hardly ever left my desk once I got to the office. My co-workers were all older than I was, so I kept to myself. They were very nice, but we had nothing in common. They didn't even live in Manhattan.

Once in a while people from the advertising agency would show up. Advertising seemed glamorous to me ever since I saw Gregory Peck in *The Man in the Gray Flannel Suit*. One day a young man I hadn't noticed before was with them. His name was Al. I had an uncle, on the wrong side of the family, named Al, who wore pinky rings and alligator shoes. This

Al wasn't like that. Just the opposite. He asked if he could use my phone even though there was an empty desk with a phone next to mine. "Yes," I said and got up.

Next time he came, he used my phone again, then looked at his watch and said, "Have you had lunch yet? Want to have a sandwich downstairs?" I was really broke from paying the psychiatrist, so I said, "Okay." We talked about what to order, the weather, and what we were eating.

When he came to the office again, he said, "Lunch?" I said, "Okay." Soon we started to meet for lunch even on days when he didn't come to our office. We still didn't talk about anything much.

Eventually, he told me he was twenty-nine years old, Jewish, and lived with his parents in Queens. He really wanted to be an artist, he said. I was surprised. He didn't look arty. He'd studied at the Art Students League, but his parents said it was more important for him to make a living than to paint so he became an art director at an advertising agency.

Al didn't seem to want anything from me. He never even tried to kiss me. The only thing he asked was that if we made a date, I show up. A couple of times I just forgot. He always called when he said he would and he always showed up. When we went to the movies, I wore my glasses.

We started to meet for dinner. He didn't mind if I

was quiet. I didn't mind if he was. I told him about the Professor and about Jeffrey. He got angry at the way they had treated me.

Sundays he'd come over to Dora's with the *New York Times* and some chocolate Danish from a special bakery in Queens. Sometimes the three of us would spend the whole afternoon doing the crossword puzzle. If Dora and I hadn't gotten dressed to go outside, he'd even walk Greco, though I knew he didn't want to.

"I've never had a boy as a friend before," I told Dora.

"He'll take good care of you," she said. I hadn't thought about him that way.

CHAPTER 15

*H*ere *I go again, I hear those trumpets blow again, all aglow again, taking a chance on love.* That Sinatra song was going through my head when Al and I were married in the spring of 1959.

Maybe Al wasn't the man of my dreams, but I thought we could have a good life. And I thought he was a really talented artist.

His mother was very upset. She didn't want her only son to marry a woman who had been married before. A woman who didn't have parents who could pay for a real wedding. When Al told me that, I didn't know who "that woman" was. Then I realized—she meant me! She thought I was marrying her son because he had $10,000 in the bank. Every time I was near her, I felt like Bette Davis in *The Little Foxes*.

The wedding was small and took place in the Rego Park Jewish Center. Neither Al nor I wore real wedding clothes, but this time when the rabbi asked us to repeat, "With this ring, you are wedded to me," we both had tears in our eyes.

After the ceremony, we went back to his parents' house in Forest Hills. Forest Hills was fancy, but his parents didn't live in the fancy part. There was a wedding cake, but it didn't have a bride and groom on top the way I'd wished. It had another bell.

Too bad my grandfather didn't come to this wedding. He would have liked the herring and the chopped liver. My grandmother was so happy, she didn't stop talking and missed the stuffed cabbage.

We didn't go on a honeymoon but used Al's $10,000 as a down payment on a house in North Stamford, Connecticut.

We had agreed that we didn't want to live in the city anymore. We both wanted to start a family—a big family—as soon as possible. And Al wanted space so he could start to paint again.

Driving back to Stamford after the ceremony, we sang our favorite song, "Our Love Is Here to Stay." Neither of us could carry a tune.

I got pregnant and quit my job.

CHAPTER 16

Me and my baby. Attached.

The baby inside me. Only me surrounding the baby. Closer than any two people could be. Closer than Siamese twins. The two of us needing nobody else. Only each other.

And I was in charge of everything.

We did everything together. We ate together. First

lightly. Then with a passion. Bananas and Rice Krispies and milk. Grilled cheese. Ketchup sandwiches on Wonder bread. Pizza. Roast chicken, fried chicken, chicken chow mein, chicken soup. Baked potatoes, hash browns, French fries. Ravioli. Spaghetti and meatballs. SpaghettiOs with franks.

Suddenly we'd be famished and drive to McDonald's. We'd wake up at 3 A.M. and devour Oreo cookies, Chips Ahoy!, Mallomars, and brownies.

We'd take long walks together. Watch TV lying on the couch together. Sleep together. We needed no one else.

How could anything else in life ever be this wonderful.

CHAPTER 17

After nine months, Al and I had our baby. It was two weeks late. I didn't want to let it out.

Al, who had dark hair and brown eyes, was thrilled with his blond-haired, blue-eyed daughter. I finally found out what sex was really for—making babies. And I knew what real love felt like—holding your baby in your arms.

We were happy. Al would leave *me* notes on my pillow. Send *me* Hallmark cards. We called each other by nicknames. He was Becky. I was Boopey.

The next year, I was pregnant again. We had a beautiful baby boy and named him David.

We were a real family. I'd drive Al to the train every morning in our Ford station wagon. Then I'd drive back to our split-level colonial and feed the children Beech-Nut and

Gerber baby food. They'd play in our paneled playroom while I polished our turquoise built-in appliances.

When the children napped, I read the Book of the Month. When they woke up, they played on the swing set in the backyard, and I watched them while I drank coffee at our redwood picnic table.

At four-thirty I'd start preparing dinner and then we'd drive to the train to get Al. After dinner, Al would play with the children. By nine-thirty we'd all be tired and ready for bed. Our springer spaniel, Happy Sam, slept at the foot of our bed.

Twice a week we'd go to the food store. Once a month we'd go to the pediatrician.

Weekends Al mowed the lawn. I weeded. One weekend we planted a sunburst locust tree in the backyard, quite a feat for Al, who grew up in Queens, and for me, from midtown Manhattan.

On Monday, February 19, 1963, both children got an intestinal virus. They were throwing up and had diarrhea all day. The doctor prescribed Kaopectate and said not to worry. Our three-year-old daughter started to get better. Eighteen-month-old David didn't. We called the doctor many times. He said it wasn't necessary to see him.

That evening David started to turn blue. We rushed

him to the emergency room. He was dehydrated, they said.
They would admit him. They told us to go home with our
daughter, not to worry, and to call in the morning.

The phone rang before morning. It was the hospital.
"Your son has expired," they said.

CHAPTER 18

The funeral was in Rego Park, on the same street as the Jewish Center where we had been married. I was six months pregnant with our third child. My obstetrician had given me some prescription pills to ease the pain. I don't think they worked. I remember the stillness of everything around me and the screaming in my head.

The funeral service didn't seem real. It couldn't be. I saw a small white box on a table with a vase filled with pink gladioli on either side. My son was in that box.

I remembered being in a room like that when I was twelve, when my mother died, except she was in a much bigger box and it was brown.

The rabbi read the Twenty-third Psalm and said words I didn't want to hear.

Before the ceremony, I told them I wanted them to open the box so I could look inside. At first they said no.

I was alone in a room with the box. I lifted the cover and saw a beautiful mannequin that looked like David. It was even wearing David's new outfit—a blue corduroy play-suit I had bought for him to wear to a party that week.

I kissed its cold, hard face and dropped one of David's wind-up toys in the box. I kept the key.

A small procession drove to the cemetery. I sat in the first car. I didn't know who else was in the car. Maybe Al.

The hole in the earth was very small. Smaller than the one we had dug to plant the sunburst locust tree. They put the box in the hole and David no longer existed.

CHAPTER 19

David was gone. And so was whatever had existed between Al and me. We couldn't look at each other. We were overcome with grief and guilt.

I kept the shades drawn in the house for months. Every time the phone rang, I shuddered. I hadn't spoken to anyone on the phone since the hospital had called. There was no one I wanted to talk to.

The new baby came. A tiny girl. I didn't know if I had anything left to give her, but when I held her, she broke my heart.

I was busy with my two daughters. Al was busy at work. We never spoke about David again. We never talked much about anything important again.

I just wanted babies. I kept getting pregnant. Six times

in seven years. But there were only five children running
around the house.

CHAPTER 20

I loved being pregnant. I loved wearing tent dresses that hid how fat I'd gotten. I even loved my obstetricians. What other man doesn't mind, actually prefers it, when you lie there passively, legs apart?

I was twenty-four years old and 336 hours pregnant when I walked into Dr. Vastola's office in Stamford.

A nurse led me into his study, where I sat biting my cuticles, until the door opened and he walked in. I was expecting someone who looked like Lionel Barrymore. Dr. Vastola was a dead ringer for James Garner. Now I knew why he was so highly recommended.

Once a month for seven months, and then once a week for four weeks, I felt I was the most important woman in his life. We had no secrets. Everything I had that was private, he touched, gently. He wanted nothing in return, except to be paid promptly. I thought he liked me because he kept giving me free samples of vaginal suppositories.

He not only cared about how I felt but about what I ate and how I slept. I had fantasies about him, including "playing doctor."

I was looking forward to the delivery and our time together. But it was 1960 and women were put to sleep during delivery. I didn't see Dr. Vastola until the next morning when he was making rounds. By then, having already delivered, I was no longer important.

My fantasy life with Dr. Vastola was relatively short. I kept imagining his starting to make love to me and then whispering, "Hmmm, what have we here? Looks like a yeast infection. I have a sample of a new suppository in my office. Back in a minute."

When we moved to New Jersey, my obstetrician was Dr. Greenfeld. He could have been a double for Walter Matthau but had the mannerisms of Groucho Marx. When he said, "Honey, take your panties off," instead of being offended, I giggled. I fully expected him to be smoking a cigar in the delivery room and bursting out, "Say the secret word and you get a boy."

During labor—it was 1964, you were supposed to stay

awake—he kept up a running monologue: "You're doing great, dollface. You're beautiful. Gimme a big push, now. That's my girl. Beautiful." When the baby's head came out, he shouted, "L'Chaim! Thank God it looks like the mother!" I was almost ready to name the new baby after him—Seymour.

Luck was with us, it was a girl.

CHAPTER 21

My life with Al was 100 percent child-centered.

There were always tears to kiss, noses to wipe, bottles to sterilize, tantrums to quiet, mittens to find, toys to fix, shoelaces to unknot, knees to bandage, lunches to make, arguments to settle. We were never without the children.

When the children went to sleep at night, I had laundry to do and clothes to iron. Al went to the room he called his studio to paint.

The years were passing quickly. Secretly, I had a crush on Mr. Rogers. He really did make me feel special. I thought he was wise and fair and always knew what to do. I was sure he could have ended the war in Vietnam if only Humphrey had made him his running mate.

I knew all the words to "Won't You Be My Neighbor," but my favorite song was "It's You I Like."

> It's you I like,
> It's not the things you wear,
> It's not the way you do your hair—
> But it's you I like.

I felt that whatever I did, however I looked, he'd still be my friend. I'd watch him take off his shoes, put on his sneakers, and zip up his sweater while I devoured a whole box of Sugar Pops.

I could only watch him when the children weren't home. They thought he was boring. They liked *The Partridge Family* and *The Brady Bunch*.

I couldn't even listen to WNEW in the car. They thought Sinatra was boring, too. Not like David Cassidy.

Al had started to paint more. Our house always smelled from dirty diapers and dog poo and oil paint and turpentine. But as the children grew bigger, his canvasses became smaller. Edvard Munch would have liked them.

He also started keeping journals. One time he left one open. I read it.

Al and I were living as strangers. Maybe each of us expected something from the other that neither of us knew how to give. Neither one of us could make the other one happy anymore. We knew that disaster could strike any sunny day.

I stayed up later and later at night so he'd be asleep before I got into bed. I knew he was getting angry, but I was grateful we never talked about it.

He was becoming more depressed, more withdrawn. I thought it was because of David. I thought it was because of me. Because I needed to lose weight. Because I bit my cuticles. Because I smoked. Because I didn't cook chicken the way he liked it.

CHAPTER 22

Since the children were mostly in school or with their friends, I needed to do something with my time. A part-time job seemed like the answer. Things weren't going so well for Al at work. A little extra money would help.

I found a job in a department store at the mall. I could be home by the time the children got home from school. "Mother's hours," they were called. Reentering the adult world meant I had to shave my legs regularly, do something with my hair, and pay attention to my nails and to what I wore.

I made friends with a co-worker, Sara. She was the first person I'd met in years who didn't know me only as Al's wife or someone's mother. Sara was in her early twenties, lived by herself, was on the pill, smoked pot regularly, and had sex

without guilt whenever she wanted, with whomever she wanted. She had every intention, she told me, of having a baby, never getting married, moving to Jackson Hole, Wyoming, and making jewelry.

It was the 1970s and I realized I had lived the past decade only in relation to my children. The hippies meant only that my daughters wanted their ears pierced. Flower children meant only that we tie-dyed T-shirts for the school fair. Vietnam meant only that the children added peace signs to their drawings.

I heard the news that Kennedy was killed while I was driving to the pediatrician. I heard that Elvis died from another mother in a Stride Rite shoe store. I heard that they'd found Marilyn's body from my pharmacist while buying St. Joseph's aspirin for children. The world seemed to be in as much turmoil as my marriage.

CHAPTER 23

One day my neighbor Grace came into the store where I was working, took one look at me, and said, "You better do something with your hair!"

She made an appointment for me with her hairdresser, Mr. Phillip at Bonwit Teller in the Short Hills Mall. It was a better mall than the one I worked in.

The affairs of certain women in the community regularly made Grace's 9 A.M. news report, which she delivered daily over coffee and cinnamon toast at the lunch counter at the deli. Grace had more scoops than Baskin-Robbins. I never suspected that Marty Howlett's mother did more than buy shoes from Rick of Rick's Shoe Box. Or that the perpetual smile on the face of the salesman at the camera store had less to do with photography and more to do with what was developing between him and Alison Sheridan's mother.

Grace got her hair "short, but not too short." Mr. Phillip styled me "parted in the middle, flip dips in front, page boy to the shoulder."

With Grace's encouragement, I started getting my hair done once a week in the evening. It was relaxing. I liked Mr. Phillip. He was good looking in a Dean Martin sort of way. He dressed like someone who sold Cadillacs and was always checking himself out in the mirror.

Mr. Phillip had his technique down pat. Even I was overtipping him. The shampoo girl would be washing my hair and Mr. Phillip would bend down and whisper in my ear, "Do you want balsam?" He had this thing for balsam. Even though a balsam rinse cost an extra $1.75, I started getting it.

Whenever Mr. Phillip put a fresh towel around my shoulders, his hands would rest on my shoulders just a moment too long. I started to look forward to his changing the towel.

I usually made the last appointment Thursday evenings so I could give the children dinner before I left. One Thursday I was late. Mr. Phillip and I were the only ones in the salon, so he had to do my shampoo. It was no ordinary hair wash. As he massaged my neck and shoulders, I only worried about how much extra an erotic shampoo might cost.

When he got to the final rinse, he leaned over and whispered, "Do you want it?" I wasn't sure if he was talking about balsam. I wasn't sure if I should feel flattered. He led me into a small back room full of bottles of Clairol. Once he grabbed my buttocks, I knew he wasn't about to teach me the beauty secrets of the stars. My hair was still wet and the towel still around my shoulders as I ran to the parking lot. I knew Mr. Phillip had the genes of a gigolo. Even though I had read *Fear of Flying*, I just didn't have lust in my jeans.

I couldn't wait to forget the experience. When I got home, I cut my Bonwit's charge card into very small pieces and never went into that Bonwit's—or any other Bonwit's— again, including the New York store, which had the best coat sales.

Things were very tense at home. Al was in a dispute with the advertising agency he worked for. They wanted him to leave. I wanted him to leave, too. To leave me. But I had no reason. He didn't drink. He didn't play around. He never hit me. He never raised his voice.

Nice girls didn't break up a marriage just because they weren't happy. My grandparents weren't happy even for ten

minutes during their fifty-five-year marriage, but they never thought about divorce.

Group therapy was big in the 1970s. My relationship with Al and with the balsam man made me realize I'd better do something, maybe try a group. They said group therapy was supposed to work faster than traditional therapy. I was getting older. I was in a hurry.

CHAPTER 25

There were eight in my group, plus Dr. Farkas, the therapist. We met Saturdays at 10 A.M. and Wednesdays at 6 P.M., for two hours each session. We weren't allowed to smoke. I didn't suspect that would end up being the easy part.

Since it was an ongoing group, everyone knew one another. There was a former alcoholic, an incest victim, a manic depressive, a closet gay, and a woman I thought was a kleptomaniac (I kept an eye on my pocketbook). The other three seemed even less happy.

One other woman started when I did. She spoke up right away. I never said anything.

After the third week, a man I had taken an instant dislike to looked at me and said, "What's your problem? You

think you're better than the rest of
us?" Everyone was staring at me.

My face got hot. I had to go to
the bathroom. My crossed leg was
swinging out of control. I had to
hold back the tears. I had to say
something.

I told them I was unhappy, but I
didn't know why. I told them Al was
very nice but I wanted to leave him. I
told them Al needed me. I told them the children needed me. I
told them I wanted to leave but couldn't. I told them I
didn't know where to go. I told them everything was fine.

I told them about Jeffrey and the Professor and the balsam
man. I told them about David. I told them about my father.

I couldn't shut up. I thought I had to tell them everything. I even told them about how I identified with Nina in
Eugene O'Neill's *Strange Interlude,* my favorite play in high
school. I began to recite:

> *My three men! . . . I feel their desires converge in me! . . .*
> *to form one complete beautiful male desire which I absorb . . .*
> *and am whole . . . they dissolve in me, their life is my life . . .*
> *I am pregnant with the three! . . . husband! . . . lover! . . .*
> *father!*

My three men, I told them, weren't husband, lover, and father but rather insatiable womanizer, ambivalent intellectual, and tormented artist.

That's when I learned that being quiet wasn't the worst thing. I had given the group the ammunition they needed to attack. Each person hit in a different place. It started with my baby voice (Didn't Jacqueline Kennedy have a baby voice? I thought) and covered everything about me, right down to my three-inch heels (Doesn't everyone want to be taller?). The one thing they all agreed on was that I deserved no sympathy.

I survived only by telling myself I'd never have to go back, never have to see any of those people again.

When Dr. Farkas finally said the session was over, I ran to the bathroom, then to my car, and I headed for the mall. Maybe I could forget the last two hours in Bloomingdale's shoe department.

Three days later, I got angry. I didn't want "those people" to think they'd gotten to me. Dr. Farkas was always saying, "Change your actions and your feelings will change." I went back. For three years.

I knew I was changing when I was able to tell Al the truth one evening, that I didn't want to be married to him anymore. He didn't have to say anything. I saw it all in his eyes.

It took all my courage to speak to him, but afterward everything went back to the way it was. That was the last thing I expected to happen.

Things never turned out as I expected.

Years later, my friend Dotty told me that people who are unhappy are people who have expectations that aren't met. When I was younger, I didn't know that if you had a good woman friend, you didn't need a therapist.

CHAPTER 26

Life continued as if I'd never said anything to Al. I did his laundry. He made the children breakfast so I could sleep a little later before work. It seemed so easy to make believe there were no problems.

Months went by. We never fought. We never hugged. We never had sex. I was waiting for a time bomb to go off, but I didn't know which one of us was going to explode first.

"It's better to be alone than to be with someone who makes you feel lonely." My grandmother knew.

CHAPTER 27

The Petersons lived up the street from us, in the best house in the neighborhood. They were a perfect couple. You could just look at their lawn and know they were perfect. They even had a little white fence with roses growing on it to hide their garbage cans.

Sometimes their children would play with mine. I'd always clean the house first.

Once I was in back of Mrs. Peterson in the check-out line at Shop Rite. I looked at what she wasn't buying—no Entenmann's, no Pop-Tarts, no frozen pizza. All the things that were in my cart.

Her hair never frizzed. Her lipstick always stayed on. Her face never broke out. Her children were popular, even though they were smart and weren't allowed to hang out at the mall. And she had the perfect husband—a good-looking doctor.

When I heard they were getting a divorce, I couldn't believe it. If a couple that perfect couldn't make it, what hope was there for me?

Al and I might have looked like the perfect couple to our neighbors. Unless they were smart enough to wonder about the crabgrass on our front lawn.

I could hear my grandmother saying, "You never know what goes on behind closed doors. Even Miss America can get hemorrhoids."

CHAPTER 28

Summer came. Since the children were in day camp, I wasn't as busy as usual. My grandmother had always said, "Keep busy, you'll stay out of trouble." For someone who had never finished grade school, my grandmother knew a lot.

When I first saw Yoram at the camp bus stop, I didn't know he was a counselor. I thought he was a divorced father. He stared at me—at every mother—as if he were trying to see what was underneath my clothes. Then he grinned, as if he'd seen.

Yoram's job at camp was to serve as a cultural representative of Israel. Until Yoram, I'd never been attracted to blond men, only Robert Redford in *The Way We Were*, before he left Barbra.

Once in a while Yoram would swagger over and tease me about having so many children. I'd tease him about having so many admirers. "And who has fallen in love with you today?" I'd ask.

One morning as I put the children on the bus, I mentioned to Yoram that I was going to the Museum of Modern Art the following day. "Good," he said, "I'll go with you." I didn't intend it to be an invitation. Or maybe I did.

The next morning as soon as the camp bus left, Yoram appeared at my car. I drove. He talked.

When we got to the museum, we went right to the cafeteria for coffee. We found a table in the garden. It started to rain. We sat in the rain looking at the Lachaise nude.

"I want to taste you," he said.

"What?"

"I want to experience you," he said.

I started to giggle. He grabbed my arm and wrestled it down, forcing it to the table. By then, we were both very wet.

"See, I have won," he said. "I have conquered you, and you must obey. Let's get out of here."

By the time we got to the car, which I'd parked at 51st Street and Eighth Avenue, we were soaked. The windows were all steamed up, and so were we.

On the drive back to New Jersey, neither one of us talked. I turned to 1010 WINS on the radio and listened to the news and weather over and over again.

A week later, Yoram left to go back to Israel and I had another pair of shoes.

Chapter 29

Up until that moment in the car, Yoram had been so much fun.

Real life wasn't fun.

Ever since high school, I'd fantasized about men I wanted to be with. They were all movie stars, except for President Kennedy.

My fantasy lovers never wanted anyone else but me. They also didn't snore at night, burp over breakfast, mess up the living room, smell up the bathroom. And they never left me.

When I was fifteen, Montgomery Clift headed my list of fantasy lovers. Other times, first place has been held by a young Marlon Brando, Gregory Peck (both young and old), Sean Connery (with and without his hair). Al Pacino headed the list once, even though he was short for me.

Cary Grant never made the list. I couldn't possibly imagine him without his clothes. We'd both be so embarrassed.

One night I couldn't fall asleep, so I started to review my list. Suddenly, it hit me: Burt Lancaster should permanently occupy first place.

The first time I saw him was in *The Killers*. Ava Gardner betrayed him in that movie. I always hated Ava. First she made love to Burt in the movies, then she married Sinatra in real life.

Yvonne De Carlo, Lizabeth Scott, Barbara Stanwyck, Joan Fontaine, Corinne Calvet, Virginia Mayo, Gina Lollobrigida, Anna Magnani, Jean Simmons, and Jeanne Moreau all made love to Burt in the movies. Deborah Kerr couldn't even tell Cary Grant she had an accident in *An Affair to Remember*, but she went crazy on the beach with Burt. He even did it with Shirley Booth, who was no beauty, so why not me?

By the time he made a pass at Susan Sarandon in *Atlantic City*, Burt and I both had gray in our hair and he still thrilled me. He deserved first place.

I should have gone to bed with Burt Lancaster videos. I might have ended up a lot happier.

CHAPTER 30

Whenever somebody commented on my big eyes, I knew I got them from my father. The last time I saw him, I was twelve. He left my sister and me the same year my mother died. Actually, he didn't leave. We did. That's not true either. My grandparents took my sister and me to live with them.

My family mourned the loss of my mother every time they got together. No one mourned the loss of my father. He must have done something terrible to make them feel that way. He never did anything terrible to me.

My father entered my life again when I least expected it.

I was buying a cameo pin for my daughter's twenty-fifth birthday in the jewelry exchange on Canal Street. "Who should I make the check out to?" I asked the man behind the counter. "To Charlie Scholar," he said.

I put the pen down. I'd heard his name a long time ago. I was shaking as I looked at the man behind the counter.

"You're going to think I'm crazy," I said, "but I think I know your name from my past. Did you ever know anyone by the name of . . ." and I said my father's name.

"He's my uncle," the man said.

"He's my father," I told him.

I couldn't handle hearing anything more just then.

It was Friday. Charlie Scholar agreed to meet me on Monday evening. On Saturday and Sunday I cursed myself a hundred times a minute for not asking the important question.

Monday evening came. I met Charlie Scholar and we made small talk for a few minutes. Then I asked him.

"Your father died two weeks ago," he said.

He showed me a recent picture of my father. He had such small eyes.

CHAPTER 31

I knew how lucky my children were to have a father who loved them, who was there for them. I loved everything having to do with the children, too. But the last four years of my marriage were miserable. I'd read that hair grows about an inch a year, a little more in the summer. One night I cut four inches off my hair.

The precarious nature of Al's job meant that I needed to get a better job. I was hired by a nonprofit community center as a communications consultant. It had become easy for me to communicate with everyone except my husband.

I'd have my own office and be paid $13,000. The most money I'd ever made.

CHAPTER 32

When I walked into the small office that would be mine, a man was sitting at my desk. He didn't look up. I introduced myself and said, "I think you're sitting at my desk. I think you're sitting in my chair."

"What are we playing, Goldilocks and the Three Bears?" he said. Then he said, "Do you know how to open this fucking thing?" He had a glue stick in his hand. "Fuck," he said, and left. This was no Cary Grant. I'd never heard a man I knew talk like that.

Later that day I found out his name was Stanley. A relative of Stanley Kowalski, no doubt. He was the arts administrator and ran the theater at the center. Rumor had it he was also the Errol Flynn of Essex County.

I always thought men had a short list when it came to women: good face, good figure, good personality, good in bed. Two out of four and they're in love. My list was even longer than Princess Turandot's when it came to men. It covered everything from being brilliant to being a Democrat. Stanley definitely didn't make the list.

Being closer to fifty than twenty, I thought that looking for love at my age was unrealistic. It was too late for someone to make me feel the way a Sinatra song did.

No one would be out there looking for me anyway. I wasn't such a bargain.

CHAPTER 33

Months went by. Everything at home was status quo. Work was going well. I was even getting used to working with Stanley. If he wasn't in his office, the first place I'd call to find him would be the steam room at the Men's Health Club at the center. His cronies in the steam room, mostly retired entrepreneurs, thought they had the answer to every problem. Never mind what advice they'd give about looking for love.

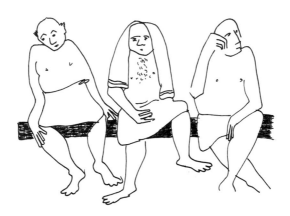

If the jokes Stanley picked up at the Men's Health Club were any indication, their advice wouldn't be much help. They tried to top each other with Henny Youngman–type one-liners: "My wife ran away with my best friend, and, let me tell you, I miss him."

I certainly had no advice to give anyone. Especially my teenaged daughters, who were having their own love problems. I wouldn't have known what to tell them, if they asked. Make sure he loves you more than you love him? Passion dies—better get your master's degree? Find out if his father plays around?

My grandmother would have said, "It's as easy to fall in love with a rich man as a poor one."

I was lucky they didn't ask.

CHAPTER 34

I always thought if I could find the right shade of lipstick, the right type of blush, mascara that didn't smudge, if my hair didn't frizz, if I could find the right outfit, my whole life would change. Something wonderful would happen.

I tried new perfumes. Different ways of tweezing my eyebrows. I'd come home from the mall with shopping bags filled with stuff from the cosmetics counters at Bloomingdale's. It didn't matter that my grandmother always said, "If beauty brought happiness, Elizabeth Taylor wouldn't need so many husbands."

On impulse one Friday night, I decided to frost my hair. When I got to Shop Rite I couldn't decide between L'Oréal and Clairol, so I bought both. I used the Clairol, timidly, and was so pleased with the results on Saturday morning that I used the L'Oréal Saturday night. Again my grandmother was right. Leave well enough alone, she used to say.

My head looked like a copper teapot, except for a large purple streak on the right side. Other than wearing hats and

scarves, or finding a convent where the nuns still wore habits, I had no idea what to do. Hairdressers were out of the question.

The children were furious. They wanted a mother who didn't stand out in a crowd. Not one whose head glowed. Al didn't notice. I survived Sunday. It was snowing and everybody was wearing a hat.

Monday morning I got to work an hour earlier so no one would see me walking through the lobby.

Midmorning, Stanley barged in while I was putting

some books away. It was too late for me to crawl under my desk. He must have seen the whole back, but not yet the purple streak.

When I turned around, he asked me about some press releases in a matter-of-fact way. I wished he'd just say something about my head and get it over with.

"What's the matter?" he asked.

"Don't be sarcastic!"

"What are you talking about?"

"My hair," I whispered.

"You look beautiful," he said.

I must have looked like a cocker spaniel who needed petting. He walked behind my desk, pulled me up out of my chair, and gave me the hug I'd been waiting for all my life.

If more men gave women hugs and told them they were beautiful when they weren't, there'd be a lot fewer divorces. My grandmother didn't say that. I did.

That night I thought a lot about Stanley. He was the opposite of every man I'd ever been attracted to.

I could relate to a man who lied to me and deceived me.

I could relate to a tormented intellectual who cared more about poetry than he did for me.

I could relate to an unfulfilled artist who seemed more interested in the color ochre than in me.

I was having trouble relating to Stanley. I kept looking for his dark side, but I couldn't find it. His feelings were all on the surface.

How could I possibly be attracted to someone like Stanley when I had always agreed with Blanche DuBois: "I don't want realism. I want magic!"

CHAPTER 35

When I was in first grade, if the roll call wasn't taken in the morning, no one would have known I was there. One day we had a substitute teacher. As she passed my desk, she stroked my hair. I thought about her many times through the years.

When Stanley hugged me, I thought about her again.

In December I asked Stanley if he wanted to go to bed with me. I could tell he was shocked. I was, too. It was the first time I had ever asserted myself. Thank God I wasn't in group therapy and didn't have to explain this mistake later.

What are you doing here, I asked myself on the silent drive to a motel in another town. That sentence seemed like a Greek chorus of grandmothers following me through life.

I had seen a comedy group once and never forgot one of their sketches. Four girls debated the merits of Phil Donahue and Richard Gere. They turned to the audience and said, "Girls, who would you rather be with? Donahue, who understands PMS, changes the baby's diapers, makes dinner, and does the dishes? Or Gere, if he pointed to his crotch and said, 'Eat this, baby!'" The audience went wild. I didn't applaud. I should have.

When we left the motel, I was floating so high I could have been in a Chagall.

What I learned in college was still true. With sex, you can't turn back. I started buying lingerie instead of underwear. I'd look at myself in a mirror, and instead of seeing who I was—Al's wife and the mother of five children—the person looking back at me was a

woman I didn't know. Hester Prynne.

I was having an affair. But to be Jewish is to be accustomed to living with guilt.

Affairs are wonderful. If only they didn't have to hurt other people. The secrecy. The longing. The passion. Having an affair is like having a very special guest, like Charlton

Heston, in your home. You're always on your best behavior. You're always charming. There are always things to talk about.

And you always look good. Stanley never saw me without mascara or with pins in my nightgown. I never had to buy him dandruff shampoo or wash his jockey shorts.

As time went by, Stanley and I both realized our needs were simpler than either of us thought. He didn't need to be a Lothario. I didn't need to be with someone who had everything I didn't.

We both had just been looking for love.

Stanley didn't have the body of a Greek god. He couldn't read poetry in French and German. He wasn't artistically gifted. He didn't look like Burt Lancaster. And it didn't matter.

I had always thought if I just acquiesced, I'd be loved. If I always said yes to Jeffrey, he'd love me. If I didn't get in the way of the Professor's work, he'd love me. If I put the ketchup bottle in Al's hand even before he asked for it, he'd love me.

Stanley didn't have these requirements. Or maybe by the time Stanley and I met, our needs and our expectations had changed.

Was I being selfish? Al's mother would definitely have said yes. My children would probably have said yes. I'm not sure what Gloria Steinem would have said. My women friends would have said, "Go for it!" My grandmother would have said, "Why look for trouble?"

I didn't need to turn on the radio to hear Sinatra. He was in my head. But even though Stanley was in an unhappy marriage, he was still somebody else's husband and I was Al's wife. Ingrid Bergman had to leave the country to be with Rossellini. Nobody thinks twice today about anything Madonna does. But I wasn't a movie star.

Even though I was a Gemini, I couldn't live a dual life. I told Al that Stanley and I had fallen in love. This time he heard me.

CHAPTER 36

If someone loves a flower, of which just one single blossom grows in all the millions and millions of stars, it is enough to make him happy just to look at the stars. He can say to himself: "Somewhere my flower is there."

I'd always believed that passage in *The Little Prince*, but I knew it wasn't true when Stanley had to go to California for two weeks. I needed my middle-aged, two-hundred-and-ten-pound flower.

Stanley and his wife separated, then divorced. Unlike the Berlin Wall, which was torn down, the wall between Al and me just crumbled.

CHAPTER 37

But still I was cautious.

New York magazine ran a special feature on psychics. Everybody at work was going to see one particular psychic named Mr. Bill in Spring Valley, New York. I made an appointment.

Mr. Bill told me that in a former life Stanley and I had been brother and sister, we had taken care of each other, and we always would. I found all that out in less than an hour and for less than $100. And I was allowed to smoke.

Because of my track record, I was still wary. My grandmother had always told me, "Get a second opinion." I went to an astrologer.

When we discussed Stanley, the astrologer told me Stanley's Sun comes exactly to my Neptune at eleven degrees.

But my Saturn is in opposition to his Sun. But everything is okay because his Jupiter triads my Sun. And Venus is in Leo in both of our charts. We had been brother and sister in a former life.

I gave her $100.

I wondered if Elizabeth Taylor had such good advice when she left Eddie Fisher for Richard Burton.

Not everything was perfect. Stanley liked classical music. I liked flea markets. But we had an arrangement. For every concert I went to, he had to go someplace he didn't want to go.

He took me to hear the Beaux Arts Trio. I took him to the Third Avenue Street Fair. He took me to hear the Tokyo String Quartet. I took him to the International Flea Market in SoHo.

CHAPTER 38

I still love Sinatra. I can be driving in my car worried about everything, then turn on WQEW. If Jonathan Schwartz is on, sooner or later, he'll play some Sinatra. Whenever I hear him sing, I start thinking about the girl I used to be and I end up thinking about Stanley.

I never would have expected when I was a senior in high school that I wouldn't find love until I was practically a senior citizen.

Stanley and I are growing old together. We still walk down the street holding hands.

We've both given up smoking. We've both started craving Chinese

food. We both could lose several pounds.

We argue about how the other one drives, about what movie to see, about what restaurant to eat in, and about how much money to spend on everything.

But we never argue about Sinatra. And there is no one in the world I would rather have next to me in bed every night. Not even Burt.

When I was younger, I never would have expected that two such imperfect people could be so perfect for each other.

My grandmother knew what she was talking about when she said, "If you have to stand on your head to make someone happy, all you can expect is a big headache."

I haven't had a headache in a long time.

P E R M I S S I O N S

The following have generously granted permission to use quotations from copyrighted works.